TOOLS FOR TEACHERS

- **ATOS:** 0.9
- **GRL:** C
- **WORD COUNT:** 40
- **CURRICULUM CONNECTIONS:** community

Skills to Teach

- **HIGH-FREQUENCY WORDS:** a, and, can, get, go, good, have, the, to, we
- **CONTENT WORDS:** book, card, computer, librarian, library, listen, story
- **PUNCTUATION:** periods, apostrophe, exclamation point
- **WORD STUDY:** long /e/, spelled *y* (*library, story*); silent *t* (*listen*); multisyllable words (*computer, librarian, library, listen*); *r*-controlled vowels (*card, computer, librarian, library, story*)
- **TEXT TYPE:** factual recount

Before Reading Activities

- Read the title and give a simple statement of the main idea.
- Have students "walk" though the book and talk about what they see in the pictures.
- Introduce new vocabulary by having students predict the first letter and locate the word in the text.
- Discuss any unfamiliar concepts that are in the text.

After Reading Activities

Encourage children to name something they'd like to learn and then discuss whether they could find the answer at a library. If so, invite them to consider how they might find it. Would they ask a librarian? Would they look for the answer in a book? Would they use a computer? Discuss their answers as a group.

Tadpole Books are published by Jump!, 5357 Penn Avenue South, Minneapolis, MN 55419, www.jumplibrary.com

Copyright ©2018 Jump. International copyright reserved in all countries. No part of this book may be reproduced in any form without written permission from the publisher.

Editorial: Hundred Acre Words, LLC **Designer:** Anna Peterson

Photo Credits: Alamy: Terrance Klassen, 2–3. Dreamstime: Photographerlondon, 4–5. iStock: blackred, cover; FangXiaNuo, 12–13; JasonDoiy, 6–7; phi2, 8–9; Rawpixel, 14–15; sdominick, 10–11. Shutterstock: Feng Yu, cover; NatashaBo, 1; Ruslan Ivantsov, 1; snapgalleria, 8–9; VectorForever, 10–11.

Library of Congress Cataloging-in-Publication Data is available at https://catalog.loc.gov or by contacting the publisher.
978-1-62031-927-7 (hardcover)
978-1-62031-928-4 (paperback)
978-1-62496-712-2 (ebook)

LIBRARY

by Erica Donner

TABLE OF CONTENTS

Let's go to the library.

librarian ·····▶

We can meet
a librarian.

We can listen
to a story.

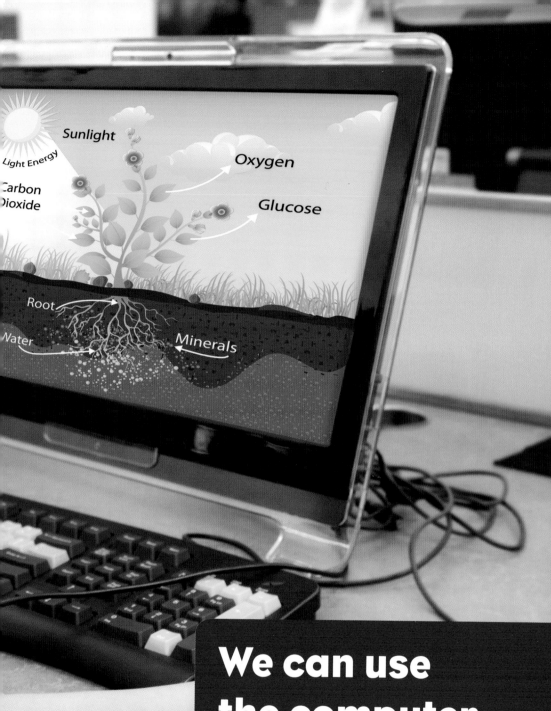

We can use the computer.

library card

Anna
Catherine

We can get a
library card.

**We can find
a good book.**

We can learn
and have fun!

WORDS TO KNOW

book

computer

librarian

library

library card

story

INDEX